"Mastering Focus in a Distracted World"

Techniques for regaining your focus amidst constant distractions

ROHAN MODY

Master Focus   Micro Series

Copyright © 2024 ROHAN MODY.
All rights reserved. This book or any portion thereof may not be reproduced or used in any manner whatsoever without the express written permission of the publisher except for the use of brief quotations in a book review.
Published by Rohan Mody, in India.
First Published, September 2024.
Publisher – KINDLE DIRECT PUBLISHING

INTRODUCTION

In a world where distractions are just a click away, maintaining focus has become both an art and a necessity. From social media notifications to the relentless buzz of emails, the modern landscape can feel overwhelming. Yet, your ability to focus has never been more critical. It's not just about completing tasks; it's about engaging deeply with your work, relationships, and personal growth.

This book is designed to help you master your focus through practical, actionable strategies. You won't find abstract theories here; instead, you'll discover techniques you can implement immediately. The goal is simple: to enhance your concentration and productivity in a tangible way.

Think of this journey as a set of tools in your toolkit. With each chapter, you'll uncover new methods to combat distractions, build a focused environment, and create a mindset that promotes sustained attention. Get ready to reclaim your focus and unlock your full potential—one small action at a time!

– Micro Self-Improvement Series –
Minimal Bite-sized self-improvement strategies that are easy to implement on a daily basis.

Crafted for individuals who like to
Read less, Do More!

Each book in the series focuses on one area of personal growth, offering quick, actionable tips for improvement.

Rohan Mody

TABLE OF CONTENTS :

Chapter 1: Understand Your Distractions   7

Chapter 2: Create a Distraction-Free Environment   10

Chapter 3: Set Clear Goals and Priorities   14

Chapter 4: Embrace the Power of Routine   17

Chapter 5: Develop Mindfulness Practices   21

Chapter 6: Limit Information Overload   25

Chapter 7: Cultivate a Growth Mindset   29

Chapter 8: Create a Distraction-Free Environment   33

Chapter 9: Leverage Technology Wisely   36

Chapter 10: Create Your Focus Masterplan   39

Conclusion: Your Focus Journey Begins Now   43

Master Focus   Micro Series

Chapter 1: Understand Your Distractions

To master focus, the first step is understanding what distracts you. Distractions can be pervasive, creeping into your day-to-day life and stealing your time and energy. By identifying these distractions, you can create targeted strategies to combat them and regain control over your attention.

Action Step 1: Conduct a Distraction Audit

Keep a distraction journal: For one week, document every time you lose focus. Note what distracted you, when it happened, and how it affected your productivity. This self-reflection will help you pinpoint patterns and identify the most common distractions in your life.

• Example: Tom, a marketing professional, realized that his biggest time-waster was social media. By tracking his usage, he discovered he spent over two hours a day scrolling mindlessly. Armed with this information, he set specific time limits for his social media use.

Reflect on the impact: After your week of tracking, take time to reflect on how these distractions affected your productivity and mental well-being. Were there specific times of day when distractions were more prevalent? Recognizing these patterns is crucial for implementing effective strategies.

Action Step 2: Identify Internal vs. External Distractions

Categorize your distractions: Create two lists—one for internal distractions (e.g., negative self-talk, stress, fatigue) and one for external distractions (e.g., noise, technology, interruptions). Understanding the source of your distractions is key to developing targeted strategies.

• Example: Rachel noticed that her internal distractions often stemmed from self-doubt, especially during high-stakes meetings. Recognizing this allowed her to prepare mentally by practising positive affirmations before important interactions.

Address the roots: Once you've identified your distractions, think about how to address them. For internal distractions, consider mindfulness practices or journaling to process your thoughts. For external distractions, think about how you can modify your environment to reduce interruptions.

Action Step 3: Create a Distraction Reduction Plan

Draft a strategy: Based on your distraction audit and categorization, draft a plan to minimize distractions. Set clear boundaries for technology use, establish focus hours, and communicate these boundaries to others.

• Example: After identifying that his co-workers often interrupted him during focused work sessions, Jake communicated his availability and established "do not disturb" hours. This simple adjustment led to a noticeable improvement in his ability to concentrate.

Implement gradually: Don't overwhelm yourself with drastic changes. Start with one or two strategies and gradually build on them. Consistency is key in developing new habits.

Chapter Summary

Understanding your distractions is the foundation for mastering your focus. By conducting a distraction audit, categorizing distractions, and creating a reduction plan, you'll begin to see improvements in your ability to concentrate. Remember, the goal is to take actionable steps that lead to tangible results. The journey to greater focus starts with awareness and small, consistent actions.

Chapter 2: Create a Distraction-Free Environment

A conducive environment is crucial for maintaining focus. Your physical space can either enhance your productivity or amplify distractions. By intentionally designing your workspace, you can foster a more focused mindset and significantly reduce interruptions.

Action Step 1: Declutter Your Space

Clear the clutter: Dedicate at least 10 minutes each day to decluttering your workspace. Remove unnecessary items that don't contribute to your work. A clean, organized space can create a sense of calm and clarity.

• Example: When Jake spent a few minutes every morning tidying his desk, he noticed a marked improvement in his ability to concentrate. Without the visual distractions of papers and random objects, he felt more focused and ready to tackle his tasks.

Organize your tools: Group similar items together and establish a system that allows you to find what you need quickly. This reduces the time spent searching for tools and minimizes distractions.

Action Step 2: Designate Focus Zones

Create specific areas for different tasks: Designate spaces in your home or office for various types of work. For example, you might have a quiet corner for deep work, a separate area for meetings, and another for creative brainstorming.

• Example: Sarah transformed a corner of her living room into a dedicated workspace. Whenever she sat there, her mind associated that space with focus and productivity, which helped her transition more easily into work mode.

Establish boundaries: Communicate with those around you about your designated focus times and spaces. Let them know when you are unavailable to minimize interruptions.

Action Step 3: Optimize Your Digital Environment

Limit digital distractions: Evaluate your digital workspace. Close unnecessary tabs, silence notifications, and use apps designed to minimize distractions. Consider tools like website blockers during focus sessions.

• Example: During her deep work hours, Lisa used a website blocker to prevent access to social media. This helped her stay focused on her tasks and significantly increased her productivity.

Organize your devices: Ensure that your digital files are well-organized. A cluttered desktop or chaotic file system can lead to frustration and distraction.

Action Step 4: Incorporate Natural Elements

Bring nature indoors: Studies show that incorporating natural elements can enhance focus and creativity. Consider adding plants or natural light to your workspace.

• Example: John added a few plants to his office and noticed that he felt more relaxed and focused. The greenery not only brightened his space but also improved his overall mood.

Use calming colors: If you have control over your workspace design, opt for calming colors like blues and greens that promote concentration.

Chapter Summary

Creating a distraction-free environment is essential for mastering focus. By decluttering your space, designing specific zones for different tasks, optimizing your digital environment, and incorporating natural elements, you can significantly enhance your ability to concentrate. The goal is to create a workspace that supports your focus and minimizes distractions, allowing you to engage deeply with your work.

Chapter 3: Set Clear Goals and Priorities

Once you understand your distractions and have optimized your environment, the next step is to establish clear goals and priorities. Focus is easier to maintain when you know precisely what you need to accomplish each day.

Action Step 1: Define Your Daily Goals

Use the SMART criteria: Each morning, take a few minutes to set SMART goals—Specific, Measurable, Achievable, Relevant, and Time-bound. This clarity helps direct your focus toward meaningful tasks.

• Example: Instead of a vague goal like "work on my project," define it as "complete the first draft of my project proposal by 3 PM." This specificity creates accountability and motivation.

Write them down: Keep your goals visible. Use a whiteboard, planner, or digital tool to track your daily objectives. Seeing your goals will remind you of what's important and help keep you on track.

Action Step 2: Prioritize Tasks Using the Eisenhower Matrix

Categorize tasks by urgency and importance: Use the Eisenhower Matrix to distinguish between what's urgent and what's important. This framework helps you focus on high-priority tasks that align with your goals.

• Example: Mark discovered he was spending too much time on tasks that felt urgent but weren't important. By prioritizing based on importance, he was able to focus on what truly mattered.

Plan your day: At the beginning of each day, review your tasks and assign them to the appropriate quadrant of the matrix. Focus on completing tasks in the "important and urgent" category first.

Action Step 3: Break Goals into Smaller Tasks

Divide larger goals into manageable steps: Breaking your goals into smaller, actionable tasks makes them less overwhelming and more achievable.

• Example: Instead of trying to write an entire report in one sitting, break it down into smaller tasks: outline the report, write the introduction, draft each section, and finalize the edits.

Set mini-deadlines: For each smaller task, set a deadline to create a sense of urgency and keep yourself accountable.

Action Step 4: Review and Adjust Regularly

Conduct a weekly review: At the end of each week, take 10–15 minutes to assess your progress. What worked well? What didn't? Use this reflection to adjust your goals and strategies for the following week.

- Example: After his weekly review, Tom realized he was more productive on days when he set fewer goals. He adjusted his approach, focusing on three significant tasks each day instead of overwhelming himself with a long list.

Chapter Summary

Setting clear goals and priorities is vital for maintaining focus. By defining daily objectives, prioritizing tasks using the Eisenhower Matrix, breaking goals into smaller steps, and regularly reviewing your progress, you can create a roadmap for success. These strategies help you stay aligned with your objectives and ensure that your focus remains directed toward meaningful actions.

Chapter 4: Embrace the Power of Routine

Establishing a consistent routine can significantly enhance your ability to focus. Routines create structure, reducing decision fatigue and allowing your brain to allocate energy toward productive tasks instead of trivial choices. When you develop habits that support your focus, you create a framework for sustained attention and productivity.

Action Step 1: Create a Morning Routine

Start your day intentionally: Dedicate the first 30 minutes of your day to a morning routine that energizes and prepares you for the day ahead. This could include activities like meditation, exercise, or reading.

• Example: Mia adopted a morning routine that included a 10-minute meditation, a brief workout, and reviewing her goals for the day.

This intentional start helped her feel grounded and ready to tackle challenges.

Limit distractions during this time: Keep your phone off and avoid checking emails or social media first thing. This protects your mental space for focused reflection and planning.

Action Step 2: Schedule Focused Work Blocks

Block out time for deep work: Identify your peak productivity hours—when you feel most alert—and schedule focused work blocks during these times. Use techniques like the Pomodoro Technique, where you work for 25 minutes and take a 5-minute break.

- Example: Kevin found that he was most productive in the early morning. By scheduling two-hour focus blocks during this time, he accomplished more and felt less overwhelmed.

Communicate your schedule: Let others know about your focus blocks to minimize interruptions. Use tools like shared calendars to indicate when you're unavailable.

Action Step 3: Establish a Wind-Down Routine

End your day on a positive note: Create a wind-down routine to signal the end of your workday. This might include reflecting on your achievements, planning for the next day, or engaging in a relaxing activity.

- Example: After work, Jessica spent 10 minutes journaling about her day and planning her top priorities for tomorrow. This routine not only helped her feel accomplished but also set her up for a productive start the next day.

Disconnect from work: Make a conscious effort to separate work from personal time. Turn off work-related notifications after hours to create mental space for relaxation and recharge.

Action Step 4: Regularly Review and Adjust Your Routine

Evaluate your routine: Every month, assess how your routine is serving you. Are there parts that are no longer effective? Are you struggling with consistency? Adjust your routine as needed to keep it relevant to your goals.

• Example: After a month, Marco realized that his early morning workout wasn't sustainable due to his changing schedule. He shifted it to lunchtime, which increased his energy levels and productivity throughout the afternoon.

Stay flexible: While routines are beneficial, it's essential to remain adaptable. Life is unpredictable, and sometimes adjustments are necessary to maintain focus and productivity.

Chapter Summary
Embracing the power of routine is a powerful strategy for enhancing focus. By creating a morning routine, scheduling focused work blocks, establishing a wind-down routine, and regularly reviewing your practices, you can cultivate an environment that supports sustained attention and productivity. Routines provide the structure needed to minimize

distractions and keep you aligned with your goals.

Chapter 5: Develop Mindfulness Practices

In a distracted world, cultivating mindfulness can be a game-changer for your ability to focus. Mindfulness involves being present in the moment, allowing you to tune out distractions and engage deeply with your tasks. By developing mindfulness practices, you can enhance your concentration and improve your overall mental clarity.

Action Step 1: Start a Mindfulness Meditation Practice

Set aside time for meditation: Dedicate 5–10 minutes each day to mindfulness meditation. Find a quiet space, sit comfortably, and focus on your breath. If your mind wanders, gently bring your focus back to your breath without judgment.

- Example: David began meditating for 10 minutes each morning. Over time, he noticed a significant reduction in his anxiety levels and an improved ability to concentrate on his work.

Use guided meditations: If you're new to meditation, consider using apps or online resources that offer guided sessions. These can help you stay focused and provide structure as you develop your practice.

Action Step 2: Practice Mindful Breathing

Incorporate mindful breathing into your day: Whenever you feel distracted or overwhelmed, take a few moments to practice mindful breathing. Close your eyes, take deep breaths, and focus solely on the sensation of your breath entering and leaving your body.

- Example: When Sarah felt stressed during a busy workday, she took a minute to practice mindful breathing. This quick reset allowed her to regain focus and approach her tasks with renewed clarity.

Set reminders: Use alarms or sticky notes to remind yourself to take mindful breaks throughout the day. Even a minute or two of focused breathing can make a difference.

Action Step 3: Engage Fully in Activities

Practice being present: Whether you're working on a project or having a conversation, strive to be fully present in the moment. Minimize distractions by putting away your phone and maintaining eye contact with others.

• Example: During team meetings, Jake made it a point to put his phone away and actively listen to his colleagues. This not only improved his focus but also strengthened his relationships with team members.

Limit multitasking: Focus on one task at a time. Multitasking can lead to decreased productivity and increased errors, making it harder to stay engaged.

Action Step 4: Reflect on Your Mindfulness Journey

Keep a mindfulness journal: At the end of each week, reflect on your mindfulness practices. What worked well? How did you feel before and after practicing mindfulness? Use these insights to refine your approach.

• Example: Mia tracked her mindfulness journey in a journal. She noted how her increased focus and decreased stress levels positively impacted her work performance.

Celebrate small wins: Acknowledge your progress, no matter how small. Each moment of mindfulness is a step toward greater focus and mental clarity.

Chapter Summary
Developing mindfulness practices is essential for mastering focus. By starting a mindfulness meditation practice, engaging in mindful breathing, being present in activities, and reflecting on your journey, you can cultivate a mindset that enhances concentration.

Mindfulness not only improves your ability to focus but also fosters a greater sense of well-being in your daily life.

Chapter 6: Limit Information Overload

In today's information-rich environment, it's easy to become overwhelmed. The constant influx of emails, news, and social media updates can scatter your focus and drain your mental energy. Learning to limit information overload is crucial for maintaining clarity and productivity.

Action Step 1: Set Boundaries for Information Consumption

Define your sources: Identify the information sources that truly add value to your life and work. Limit your consumption to these sources and unsubscribe from anything that doesn't contribute meaningfully.

• Example: Alex realized he was subscribed to numerous newsletters that cluttered his inbox. By unsubscribing from those that didn't align with his goals, he significantly reduced the amount of information he had to sift through daily.

Establish information intake times: Set specific times during the day to check emails and social media rather than doing it sporadically. This helps you maintain focus on your primary tasks without constant interruptions.

Action Step 2: Create a Digital Detox Plan

Schedule regular breaks from technology: Dedicate specific times each week to unplug from your devices. Use this time for activities that promote relaxation and creativity, such as reading a book, going for a walk, or engaging in a hobby.

• Example: During weekends, Lisa implemented a digital detox, disconnecting from all screens for several hours. This break helped her recharge and return to work with renewed focus.

Limit social media use: Set boundaries for social media consumption. Consider using apps that track your usage and help you stay accountable to your limits.

Action Step 3: Practice the 80/20 Rule

Focus on the vital few: Apply the Pareto Principle (80/20 rule) to your information consumption. Identify the 20% of information that provides 80% of the value. Concentrate on these key areas and let go of the rest.

• Example: Marco discovered that only a few news sources kept him informed without overwhelming him. By focusing on these, he felt more knowledgeable and less stressed.

Streamline your reading list: Curate your reading list to include only the most relevant and valuable resources. Set a goal for how many articles or books you'll read each month, ensuring that they align with your personal or professional goals.

Action Step 4: Review Your Information Diet Regularly

Conduct regular audits: Every month, review your information sources and consumption habits. Are there new distractions creeping in? Adjust your boundaries as needed to maintain a healthy information diet.

• Example: At the end of each month, Sarah reviewed her news and social media subscriptions. This reflection allowed her to keep her information intake in check.

Stay adaptable: Information overload is an ongoing challenge. Stay open to adjusting your strategies as needed to keep your focus sharp and your mind clear.

Chapter Summary

Limiting information overload is essential for maintaining focus in a distracted world. By setting boundaries for information consumption, creating a digital detox plan, practising the 80/20 rule, and regularly reviewing your habits, you can protect your mental space and enhance your ability to concentrate. A healthier information diet leads to improved focus and productivity.

Chapter 7: Cultivate a Growth Mindset

A growth mindset—the belief that abilities and intelligence can be developed—can significantly impact your ability to focus and succeed. When you adopt a growth mindset, you become more resilient in the face of challenges, viewing them as opportunities for growth rather than obstacles.

Action Step 1: Challenge Limiting Beliefs

Identify negative self-talk: Pay attention to the internal dialogue that arises when you encounter difficulties. Are you telling yourself you can't focus or that you're not capable? Recognize these limiting beliefs as barriers to your growth.

• Example: Emma often told herself, "I'm just not good at staying focused." After realizing this, she reframed her thoughts to, "I can improve my focus with practice." This simple shift encouraged her to take action rather than retreat.

Replace negativity with positivity: When you catch yourself in a negative thought pattern, consciously replace it with a positive affirmation. Affirmations can help reinforce a growth mindset and build your confidence.

• Example: Every morning, Sam recited affirmations like, "I embrace challenges and learn from them," which helped him approach his work with a renewed sense of possibility.

Action Step 2: Embrace Challenges as Learning Opportunities

Reframe challenges: Instead of viewing obstacles as setbacks, see them as chances to learn and grow. Ask yourself, "What can I learn from this experience?"

• Example: When James struggled with a complex project, he viewed it as a valuable learning opportunity. Instead of feeling defeated, he sought help and learned new skills that enhanced his focus and efficiency.

Celebrate effort, not just outcomes: Acknowledge the effort you put into tasks, regardless of the outcome. This fosters a growth mindset and encourages persistence.

Action Step 3: Surround Yourself with Growth-Minded People

Build a supportive network: Surround yourself with individuals who encourage growth and development. Engage in conversations that inspire you to expand your thinking and challenge your limits.

• Example: Sophia joined a local group focused on personal development. The supportive environment helped her maintain motivation and reinforced her commitment to continuous improvement.

Learn from others' successes: When you see someone achieving success, instead of feeling envious, ask yourself what you can learn from their journey. This shift in perspective encourages you to adopt new strategies and practices that can enhance your focus.

Action Step 4: Set Growth-Oriented Goals

Create specific, achievable goals: Instead of setting vague objectives, create SMART (Specific, Measurable, Achievable, Relevant, Time-bound) goals that encourage you to stretch your abilities.

• Example: Instead of saying, "I want to be more focused," set a goal like, "I will complete two hours of focused work each day for the next month." This clarity helps you take actionable steps toward improvement.

Track your progress: Regularly review your progress towards your goals. Celebrate milestones and adjust your strategies as needed to stay on track.

Chapter Summary

Cultivating a growth mindset is crucial for mastering focus in a distracted world. By challenging limiting beliefs, embracing challenges as learning opportunities, surrounding yourself with growth-minded individuals, and setting growth-oriented goals, you can create a mindset that supports sustained focus and productivity. A growth mindset fosters resilience and encourages you to embrace the journey of continuous improvement.

Chapter 8: Create a Distraction-Free Environment

Your physical environment plays a significant role in your ability to focus. A cluttered or chaotic space can lead to distraction and decreased productivity. By creating a distraction-free environment, you can enhance your focus and foster a mindset conducive to deep work.

Action Step 1: Declutter Your Workspace

Clear your desk: Spend 10–15 minutes decluttering your workspace. Remove items that don't serve a purpose or that cause distractions.

• Example: Laura took the time to organize her desk, removing unnecessary paperwork and personal items. With a clean workspace, she found it easier to concentrate on her tasks.

Implement a "one in, one out" rule: For every new item you bring into your workspace, consider removing something else. This helps maintain a clutter-free environment over time.

Action Step 2: Designate a Focus Zone

Create a specific area for focused work: Whether it's a corner of your home or a designated room, establish a space where you only engage in tasks that require deep concentration.

• Example: Max set up a home office dedicated solely to focused work. By reserving this space for important tasks, he trained his brain to associate it with productivity.

Personalize your focus zone: Decorate your focus zone with items that inspire you, such as motivational quotes or images. This personalization can create a positive atmosphere that enhances your focus.

Action Step 3: Control Environmental Distractions

Manage noise levels: Identify sources of noise that distract you and take steps to minimize them. This could involve using noise-cancelling headphones, playing ambient music, or utilizing white noise machines.

• Example: Nina found that listening to instrumental music while she worked helped drown out distractions and kept her focused for longer periods.

Limit visual distractions: Position your computer screen away from windows or other areas that may divert your attention. If possible, use curtains or blinds to control the amount of light and visual stimuli in your workspace.

Action Step 4: Optimize Your Digital Environment
Organize your digital workspace: Clean up your desktop, organize files into folders, and delete any unnecessary apps. A cluttered digital workspace can be just as distracting as a physical one.

• Example: Ryan spent an hour organizing his digital files, which made it easier to find what he needed quickly. This small change helped him maintain focus and efficiency.
Limit browser distractions: Use browser extensions to block distracting websites or limit your time on social media during focused work sessions. This reduces the temptation to divert your attention.

Chapter Summary

Creating a distraction-free environment is essential for enhancing focus and productivity. By decluttering your workspace, designating a focus zone, controlling environmental distractions, and optimizing your digital space, you can foster an atmosphere conducive to deep work. A well-structured environment supports your ability to concentrate and engage fully in your tasks.

Chapter 9: Leverage Technology Wisely

Technology can be both a blessing and a curse when it comes to focus. While it offers tools for productivity, it can also create distractions. Learning to leverage technology wisely allows you to enhance your focus and streamline your workflow.

Action Step 1: Utilize Productivity Apps

Explore productivity tools: Research and experiment with productivity apps designed to help you manage tasks, set reminders, and track your time. Find tools that align with your working style.

- Example: Sarah discovered a task management app that helped her prioritize her daily tasks and set reminders for deadlines. This organization improved her focus and reduced her overwhelm.

Limit app notifications: Disable non-essential notifications from productivity apps. This minimizes interruptions and allows you to stay focused on your tasks.

Action Step 2: Implement Time-Tracking Techniques

Track your time: Use time-tracking apps or simple timers to monitor how much time you spend on various tasks. This helps you identify patterns and areas for improvement.

- Example: After tracking her time for a week, Emily realized she spent too much time on social media during work hours. This insight encouraged her to limit her usage during focus sessions.

Analyse your productivity patterns: At the end of each week, review your time-tracking data. Identify which tasks consumed the most time and whether they aligned with your priorities.

Action Step 3: Use Automation to Streamline Tasks

Identify repetitive tasks: Look for tasks in your workflow that can be automated, such as email filtering or scheduling. Automating these tasks frees up mental energy for more focused work.

- Example: Mark used automation tools to filter and organize his emails, allowing him to focus on important messages without constant interruptions.

Set up recurring reminders: Use digital calendars to schedule regular reminders for tasks that need to be completed consistently. This helps you stay organized and accountable.

Action Step 4: Take Technology Breaks

Schedule regular tech breaks: Dedicate time to step away from screens and engage in non-digital activities. This prevents burnout and enhances your ability to focus when you return.

• Example: After every hour of screen time, Lisa took a 10-minute break to stretch, drink water, or go for a short walk. This routine helped her maintain her energy levels throughout the day.

Reflect on your technology usage: At the end of each week, evaluate how technology impacted your focus. Are there tools that hinder your productivity? Adjust your usage as necessary.

Chapter Summary

Leveraging technology wisely is essential for mastering focus. By utilizing productivity apps, implementing time-tracking techniques, using automation to streamline tasks, and taking regular technology breaks, you can enhance your ability to concentrate and work efficiently. Technology should support your focus, not distract from it.

Chapter 10: Create Your Focus Masterplan

Now that you've learned various techniques for enhancing focus, it's time to create a personalized focus master plan. This plan will integrate the strategies you've discovered throughout the book and help you maintain a sustainable focus in your daily life.

Action Step 1: Assess Your Current Focus Practices

Evaluate your current habits: **Take time to reflect on your existing focus practices. What techniques have worked for you? What distractions continue to challenge your ability to concentrate?**

• **Example:** Sarah assessed her current habits and found that while she had a morning routine, she struggled to maintain focus during the afternoon. This insight allowed her to strategize improvements.

Action Step 2: Set Specific Focus Goals

Define your focus goals: Based on your assessment, set specific goals for improving your focus. These could include goals related to productivity, mindfulness, or technology usage.

- **Example:** Define your focus goals: Based on your assessment, set specific goals for improving your focus. These could include goals related to productivity, mindfulness, or technology usage.

- Example: Emma set a goal to increase her daily focused work time to four hours by implementing the Pomodoro Technique and minimizing distractions during those periods. This clear objective gave her a target to work towards.

Action Step 3: Design Your Daily Focus Routine

Integrate effective strategies into your routine: Develop a daily schedule that incorporates the focus-enhancing techniques you've learned, such as morning rituals, scheduled breaks, and technology limits.

- Example: David designed a daily plan where he dedicated the first hour of work to deep tasks, followed by short breaks for mindful breathing. He also allocated specific times for checking emails to avoid constant interruptions.

Stay flexible: While routines are important, remain adaptable. If something isn't working, don't hesitate to tweak your approach. Focus is a skill that can evolve with practice.

Action Step 4: Build Accountability into Your Plan

Share your goals with others: Discuss your focus goals and strategies with friends, family, or colleagues. Having someone to share your progress with can increase accountability and motivation.

• Example: Jake joined a productivity group where members shared their goals and progress weekly. This accountability helped him stay committed to his focus practices.
Regularly review your progress: Set aside time each week to evaluate your focus master plan. Are you meeting your goals? What adjustments can you make to improve?

Action Step 5: Celebrate Your Achievements

Acknowledge your progress: Take time to celebrate the small wins along the way. Recognizing your efforts reinforces positive behaviour and motivates you to continue.

• Example: After achieving a week of consistent focused work sessions, Mia treated herself to a night out with friends. Celebrating milestones helped her stay motivated and committed to her focus journey.

Reflect on your journey: As you progress, reflect on how far you've come. Consider writing down your thoughts and feelings about your focus improvements and the impact they've had on your life.

Chapter Summary

Creating your focus master plan is the final step in mastering focus in a distracted world. By assessing your current practices, setting specific goals, designing a daily routine, building accountability, and celebrating your achievements, you can develop a sustainable strategy for maintaining focus. Your master plan will serve as a guide, helping you navigate distractions and enhance your productivity over time.

Conclusion: Your Focus Journey Begins Now

Mastering focus in a distracted world is an ongoing journey, not a destination. You've equipped yourself with essential tools to enhance your concentration, manage distractions, and foster a productive mindset. Each chapter has provided actionable steps designed to help you implement these strategies in your daily life.

As you embark on this journey, embrace the challenges and celebrate your successes. Keep refining your strategies, stay adaptable, and remember that focus is a skill developed through consistent practice and dedication.

So, as you close this book, ask yourself: What is the one specific action you will take today to reclaim your focus? Will you implement a new technique from this book, set aside time for deep work, or establish a distraction-free zone?

Your focus journey starts now—

Take That First Step!

Rohan Mody

www.ingramcontent.com/pod-product-compliance
Lightning Source LLC
Chambersburg PA
CBHW030517220526
45464CB00006B/2838